WE THE PEOPLE

SOLDIER AND FOUNDER
ALEXANDER HAMILTON

by Michael Burgan

Content Adviser: Richard Bell,
Department of History,
University of Maryland

Reading Adviser: Alexa L. Sandmann, Ed.D.,
Professor of Literacy, College and Graduate School
of Education, Health, and Human Services,
Kent State University

Compass Point Books ✦ Minneapolis, Minnesota

Compass Point Books
151 Good Counsel Drive
P.O. Box 669
Mankato, MN 56002-0669

 This book was manufactured with paper containing at least 10 percent post-consumer waste.

On the cover: Alexander Hamilton addresses a crowd in New York at King's College in 1775.

Photographs ©: The Granger Collection, New York, cover, 4, 11, 13, 17; Library of Congress, 5, 6, 12, 15, 25, 29, 31; Bill Bachmann/Alamy, 8; Mary Evans Picture Library, 9; Corbis, 19; Rare Book and Special Collection Division, Library of Congress, 22; The Bridgeman Art Library/Getty Images, 23; Architect of the Capitol, 27; Kean Collection/Getty Images, 32; Line of Battle Enterprise, 34; U.S. Senate Collection/*John Adams* by Eliphalet Frazer Andrews (detail), 36; Private Collection/Peter Newark American Pictures/The Bridgeman Art Library, 37; North Wind Picture Archives, 39; Wikimedia/Nathan Stringer, 41.

Editor: Mari Bolte
Page Production: Bobbie Nuytten
Photo Researcher: Svetlana Zhurkin
Cartographer: XNR Productions, Inc.
Library Consultant: Kathleen Baxter

Art Director: LuAnn Ascheman-Adams
Creative Director: Joe Ewest
Editorial Director: Nick Healy
Managing Editor: Catherine Neitge

Library of Congress Cataloging-in-Publication Data
Burgan, Michael.
 Soldier and founder : Alexander Hamilton / by Michael Burgan.
     p. cm. — (We the People)
 Includes index.
 ISBN 978-0-7565-4116-3 (library binding)
1. Hamilton, Alexander, 1757–1804—Juvenile literature. 2. Statesmen—United States—Biography—Juvenile literature. 3. United States—History—Revolution, 1775–1783—Juvenile literature. 4. United States—Politics and government—1783–1809—Juvenile literature. I. Title.
 E302.6.H2B86 2009
 973.4092—dc22
 [B]   2008037634

Visit Compass Point Books on the Internet at *www.compasspointbooks.com*
or e-mail your request to *custserv@compasspointbooks.com*

Table of Contents

1 Building a New Government

Throughout the summer of 1787, some of the best minds in the United States gathered in Philadelphia. Their goal was to improve the country's national government. Just four years before, the United States had gained its independence from

For four months, 55 delegates from 12 states met to discuss the future of the United States.

Britain after winning the Revolutionary War. Since then, the

13 states had sometimes quarreled with each other. At times,

they had refused to give money to Congress, the existing national

government, to run the country.

Alexander Hamilton was one of the leaders who called

for this Philadelphia

convention. Even

before the war ended,

Hamilton thought

that the United States

needed a stronger

national government.

Americans, he wrote in

1781, "ought without

delay, to enlarge the

powers of Congress."

Alexander Hamilton's notes for his five-hour speech to the convention explain his vision for the country's new government.

Alexander Hamilton is known as one of the
Founding Fathers of the United States.

In particular, the government had to be able to raise money through taxes and to control foreign trade.

In 1787, 12 out of 13 states sent delegates to the Philadelphia convention. The delegates debated several plans for creating a new national government.

By the time the convention ended in September, they had written the Constitution. This document spelled out the form of the new government and its powers. Hamilton then worked hard to make sure the states approved the Constitution.

During the Revolutionary War, Hamilton had fought bravely for American freedom from Britain. Later, in the government created by the Constitution, he served as the first secretary of the Treasury Department. George Washington, the first president, trusted Hamilton and his skills. He gave Hamilton more power than any other secretary in the new government.

Having so much power and influence, Hamilton sometimes made enemies. Some people opposed his plans, thinking they favored the wealthy. Others thought he was too concerned with winning fame for himself. Yet Hamilton impressed many people with his intelligence and love of his country. He worked hard to do what he thought was right.

2 From St. Croix to America

*A*lexander Hamilton's life began on the small island of Nevis, located in the Caribbean Sea. He was born there January 11, 1755. His parents, Rachel Faucett Lavien and James

Alexander Hamilton's home on Nevis, built in 1680, was destroyed by an earthquake in 1840. It has since been rebuilt.

Hamilton, were not married. At the time, most Americans and Europeans looked down on the children of unmarried parents. Throughout his life, Hamilton worked hard to prove his worth and talents to others.

In 1765, the Hamilton family moved to St. Croix, another island in the Caribbean. In much of the Caribbean, the economy was built on slavery. Enslaved people, taken by force from Africa, raised such crops as sugar-cane and coffee.

More than 3 million African slaves were brought to the Caribbean until the slave trade became illegal in 1807. Slavery itself existed in the Caribbean until 1834.

Hamilton saw how harshly slaves were treated, and as an adult he opposed slavery.

On St. Croix, the Hamiltons struggled to survive. James Hamilton made little money as a merchant, and he left his family when Alexander was about 11. His mother then ran a small shop, while Alexander took a job as a clerk for a shipping company. He never spent much time in school, though he loved reading books.

When Alexander was 13, his mother died. Alexander and his brother, James, had no money and briefly lived with a cousin. When the cousin died about a year later, Alexander moved in with the family of his friend, Edward Stevens. Alexander wrote a letter to Edward saying he did not want to spend his life as a clerk. "I would willingly risk my life though not my character to exalt [raise] my station [position in society]."

At the shipping company, Alexander impressed the two owners with his skills. By the time he was 16, he was running

Clerks worked at the counting room of a shipping company.

the company when the men were away. Hamilton also became friendly with Hugh Knox, a minister who arrived in St. Croix in 1772. Knox wanted to help poor but smart young men like Hamilton make the most of their talents. Knox and local merchants arranged for Hamilton to go to college in America.

In the fall of 1772, Hamilton sailed for Boston. From there he went to New Jersey, hoping to study at the College of

Hamilton had to travel more than 1,500 miles (2,414 kilometers) by sea to reach Boston.

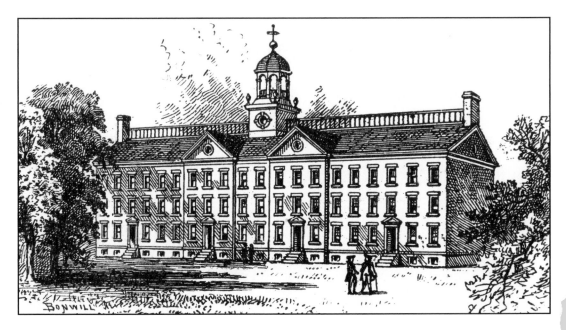

King's College was founded in 1754 by King George II. It is the oldest university in New York and the fifth oldest in the United States.

New Jersey (now called Princeton University). First, though, he had to learn Latin and Greek. All educated people of the time were expected to know these languages. Hamilton was eager to enter college, so he raced through his courses. Then he asked to take courses at the College of New Jersey at the same fast pace. School leaders said no, so Hamilton turned to King's College (now Columbia University) in New York City. The officials there agreed to let Hamilton complete courses as quickly as he liked.

3 Revolution

*A*lexander Hamilton arrived at King's College in 1773. At the time, New York was one of 13 American colonies under British control. Since 1764, the British had tried to raise money taxing the colonies. Many Americans, called patriots, resisted these efforts. The colonists who supported the British were called loyalists. Hamilton quickly chose the patriot side and began using his knowledge and writing skills to publicly support it.

During the fall of 1774, patriot leaders from various colonies met in Philadelphia. They discussed how they should work together against the British. The meeting was called the First Continental Congress. The members did not want independence from Britain. Instead, they wanted an end to Britain's policies that threatened their freedom. Hamilton wrote articles defending the Continental Congress and its views. "The Americans are entitled to freedom," he said. No group, such as the British Parliament, should claim power over another, he said, unless the second group agreed to give power to the first. The Americans, he wrote, "have not ... empowered the British Parliament to make laws for them."

In April 1775, fighting between Massachusetts' patriots and British soldiers erupted in the towns of Lexington and Concord. Soon other colonies were sending troops and supplies to help the patriots there. In New York, a group of local soldiers called a militia prepared for war. Hamilton joined the

A

FULL VINDICATION

OF THE

Meafures of the Congrefs,

FROM

The Calumnies of their Enemies;

In Answer to

A L E T T E R,

Under the Signature of

A. W. F A R M E R.

WHEREBY

His *Sophiftry* is expofed, his *Cavils* confuted, his *Artifices* detected, and his *Wit* ridiculed;

IN

A General Address

To the Inhabitants of America,

AND

A Particular Addrefs

To the Farmers *of the Province of New-York.*

Veritas magna eft & prævalebit.
Truth is powerful, and will prevail.

N E W - Y O R K:
Printed by James Rivington. 1774.

In 1774, Hamilton wrote A Full Vindication of the Measures of the Congress, *which defended the Continental Congress.*

militia, and the next year he was named captain of an artillery unit. The unit's cannons were soon in action as the war spread to New York.

During the summer of 1776, the British sent tens of thousands of soldiers to New York City. American troops led by George Washington were camped on Long Island, just across from the city. Through the summer, the two armies battled in and around the area. Hamilton and his men fought in several of the battles. The Americans, however, did poorly and were forced to retreat to New Jersey. By that time, the 13 American colonies had declared their independence and were fighting for their freedom from Britain.

That December, the Americans finally won a major victory, defeating the British in Trenton. Early in 1777, the patriots won again at Princeton. Hamilton fought in both battles. At Princeton, he ordered his men to cover the wheels of their cannons with rags. The rags helped soften the noise of the rolling wheels so the enemy would not hear them approach.

Hamilton's skill and bravery impressed General Washington. In March, he asked Hamilton to serve as his top aide. Hamilton also received the rank of lieutenant colonel. In his new role, Hamilton wrote reports and letters for Washington.

Hamilton proved himself in the Continental Army, fighting in the Battles of Long Island, Trenton, and White Plains.

The 13 original colonies streched from Georgia to present-day Maine.

He also made trips to gather information or meet with other offi-

cers. Washington and Hamilton became close friends.

During the war, Hamilton had little time for dances and

other social events. But at an event at George Washington's headquarters, he met Elizabeth Schuyler. Her father, Philip, was a wealthy New York landowner and political leader. Hamilton and Schuyler married at the Schuyler home in December 1780, while the war was still going on.

Both Hamilton's wedding and the celebration that followed took place in the Schuyler mansion.

By that time, most of the military action was in the south. After more than three years as Washington's aide, Hamilton wanted to actively fight again. In February 1781, a small argument between him and the general led Hamilton to quit as Washington's aide. He then received a position commanding New York troops.

In October, Hamilton again served under Washington, this time at Yorktown, Virginia. Hamilton once again fought bravely, and he and his men captured a small British fort. With help from France, the Americans defeated the British at Yorktown. The victory led the British to end the war and give the Americans their freedom. The war officially ended in 1783.

4 Troubles for the Country

*E*ven while serving in the army, Alexander Hamilton continued to write about politics. His job with General Washington gave him a good look at the relationship between the states and the Second Continental Congress. This Congress ran the national government during most of the Revolution. Congress, Hamilton wrote in 1780, lacked the power it needed to run the country well. The states, he said, had "too much influence in the affairs of the army," which hurt the war effort. He also believed the states did not always work together to achieve a common goal. For these and other reasons, Hamilton worried about the future of the country.

At that time, the United States did not have an official national government approved by the states. In 1777, Congress had written a document called the Articles of Confederation.

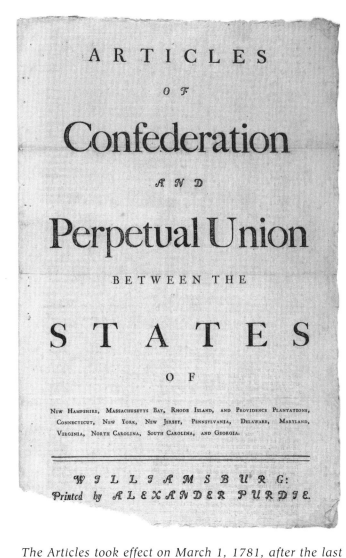

The Articles took effect on March 1, 1781, after the last of the 13 states approved the document.

It outlined the shape of the national government. The Articles were not ratified until 1781, several months before the Battle of Yorktown. Under the Articles, Congress still lacked the power over the states that Hamilton thought it needed.

At the end of 1781, Hamilton left the military and returned to New York. He began to study law and briefly served in Congress. His fears about the weakness of the national government continued to grow. Over the next few years,

Hamilton worked as a lawyer and helped found the Bank of New York. He also set time aside for politics. In 1786, he was elected to the New York Assembly, which made laws for the state. He was soon chosen to represent New York at a convention in Annapolis, Maryland.

The idea for the meeting came from James Madison of Virginia. Like Hamilton, he thought the Articles of Confederation had created a weak national government. At the Annapolis Convention, delegates from five states agreed that Congress

James Madison (1751–1836)

should hold another convention to make changes to the Articles and strengthen the government. They suggested that the convention be held in Philadelphia in May 1787.

Hamilton was one of three New Yorkers chosen to go to the Philadelphia convention. By the time he arrived for the meeting, trouble had broken out in several states. Many soldiers returned from the war and quickly went into debt. States added to citizens' problems by raising taxes. In several states, groups of farmers protested the taxes, and violence broke out between rebels and the militia in Massachusetts. Meanwhile, Congress had not been able to find enough volunteers to help the militia. More people joined Hamilton and Madison in seeing the need for a stronger national government.

5

The Constitution

*I*n May 1787, delegates from every state but Rhode Island

began meeting in Philadelphia. Through the summer, they

discussed how the new government

should work. Alexander

Hamilton's ideas startled

some delegates. More

than some leaders of

the time, Hamilton

did not trust people

to always do what was

right for the country as a

whole. He thought only the

smartest men, with the

best sense of right and

Alexander Hamilton believed that ordinary people could not be trusted to elect leaders for the country.

wrong, should rule. He included himself among those people. Hamilton did want to do what was best for the country, but some Americans disliked his desire to keep power away from average citizens by limiting their role in the government.

In his speech, Hamilton called for electing the head of the executive branch of the government for life. The head of that branch became known as the president. Hamilton also wanted the president to choose the governors of the states. Hamilton's plan was too extreme for most delegates, who felt that the president would be too much like a king. Americans had fought the Revolutionary War to escape British rule. They did not want to give that much power to the new national government.

When the convention ended in September, Hamilton supported the Constitution that the delegates had approved. This document outlined the new government and its basic laws. The Constitution created what is called a federal government, with

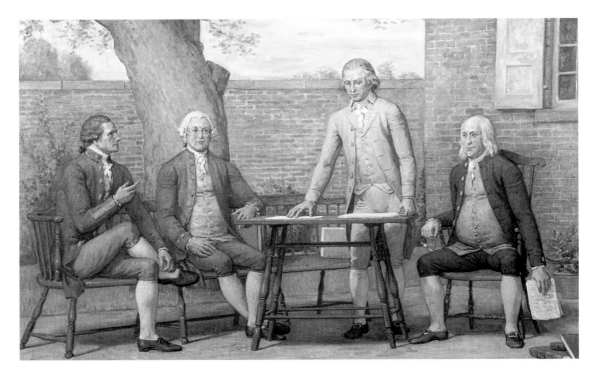

Delegates Alexander Hamilton (from left), James Wilson, James Madison, and Benjamin Franklin met often to discuss the future of the government.

power shared among the states, the national government, and the people as a whole. The national, or federal, government was divided into three branches. The legislative branch makes laws for the country, while the executive branch carries out the laws. The judicial branch makes sure the laws are carried out fairly and do not violate the Constitution.

For the new government to take effect, nine of the 13 states had to ratify the Constitution. In each state, people argued for and against it. The ones who supported the Constitution were called Federalists. Their opponents, known as the Anti-Federalists, thought the new government took away too much power from the states. Hamilton quickly became one of the leading Federalists in the country.

In the fall of 1787, he began writing a series of articles supporting the Constitution. He worked with James Madison and a New York lawyer named John Jay. Their articles arguing for the Constitution were later collected in a book called the *The Federalist* (later known as *The Federalist Papers*). Hamilton wrote more than half the articles. He said that the Constitution was "necessary to the public safety and prosperity [wealth]." Only a strong federal government could raise an army and defend the country if it were attacked. That government could also create laws that would help businesses grow and end problems with debt.

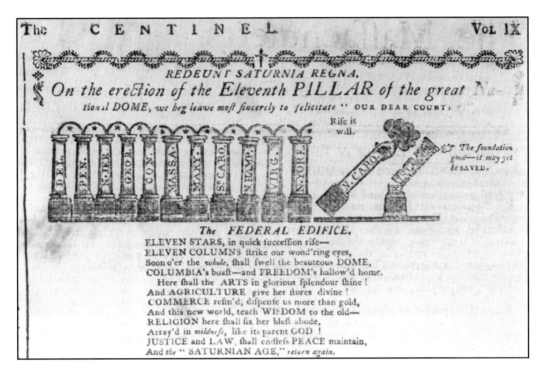

A series of political cartoons representing the ratification of the Constitution was published in the Massachusetts Centinel *in 1788.*

In December 1787, Delaware became the first state to ratify the Constitution. The following summer, New Hampshire became the ninth state, meaning the new government would take effect. Still, Hamilton thought it was important for New York, his adopted state, to approve the Constitution. He worked hard to win support among the men who would vote on the ratification. In the end, the Federalists won in New York by just three votes.

6 Serving the Government

When it came time to choose a president, Alexander Hamilton thought his old friend George Washington was the best choice. The voters agreed, and Washington began his term on April 30, 1789. Washington knew Hamilton's strengths, especially in finance. He soon named Hamilton secretary of the Treasury Department. This department handles the government's collection of taxes and pays its bills.

Hamilton took the job knowing both the federal government and the states were in debt. He wanted to pay off those debts so it would become easier for the country to borrow money in the future. Hamilton also thought the federal government should pay the states' debts. He hoped this would help win support for the new government.

Not everyone welcomed Hamilton's ideas. Some states,

such as Virginia, had already paid their debts from the

Revolutionary War. They didn't think it was fair for other states'

debts to be paid by the federal government. Hamilton worked

with Thomas Jefferson, a Virginian, to win the state's support for

his plan. The U.S. government agreed to build its new capital

along the Potomac River, near Virginia. The state's members

George Washington gave his first inaugural address in New York.

in Congress then agreed to accept Hamilton's debt plan.

As secretary of the treasury, Hamilton also created the first national bank, the Bank of the United States. Once again, he had to fight lawmakers who opposed him. These critics said the Constitution did not give the government specific powers to start a bank. Hamilton argued that Congress had the right to do some things not spelled out in the Constitution if they were necessary

The First Bank of the United States was approved in 1791. Construction of the Philadelphia bank was completed in 1797.

or useful for the government to run smoothly. This idea was later accepted by the U.S. Supreme Court, the most powerful court in the country.

For several years, Hamilton wrote reports, called for new taxes on certain items, and promoted trade and manufacturing. He always wanted to find new ways to strengthen the U.S. economy. Not everyone, though, welcomed his efforts. Two men who came to oppose him were Thomas Jefferson and James Madison. Jefferson was the country's secretary of state. In that position, he advised President Washington on foreign affairs. Jefferson thought that the economy should be centered on farming. He opposed Hamilton's efforts to promote manufacturing and trade. Jefferson also believed Hamilton was seeking too much power for the new federal government. He thought Hamilton's actions would destroy the country. Madison, who had worked with Hamilton on *The Federalist Papers*, now agreed with Jefferson.

Members of Washington's Cabinet included (from left) Henry Knox, Thomas Jefferson, Edmund Randolph, and Alexander Hamilton.

The split between Hamilton and the other two men led to

the first political parties in the United States. Lawmakers and

voters who supported Hamilton were called Federalists. Jefferson,

Madison, and their supporters were known as Republicans. (This

party was not the same as today's Republican Party.) Foreign affairs also divided the two groups. Hamilton and the Federalists wanted close ties with Britain. The Republicans did not trust the British and sought better relations with France.

Relations between Hamilton and Jefferson turned bitter. Hamilton said that it was Jefferson who wanted to "destroy the credit and honor of the nation." Each of the men was connected to newspapers. The editors of papers that supported Hamilton attacked Jefferson, while Jefferson's papers did the same to Hamilton. One of Jefferson's supporters accused Hamilton of using government money illegally. Hamilton proved that the charge was false. The attacks, though, seemed to weaken his desire to serve in government. He also felt the need to make more money to support his growing family. (His first child, Philip, was born in 1782. Seven siblings would follow.) Early in 1795, Hamilton left his position as secretary of the treasury and returned to New York City.

7 Last Struggles

*E*ven out of government office, Alexander Hamilton remained active in politics. While practicing law, he wrote articles and letters that supported Federalist views. He also became involved in military matters again. In 1798, war seemed possible between France and the United States. John Adams was now president, and he asked George Washington to lead the military. Washington said he

John Adams (1735–1826)

would, but only if Adams gave Hamilton a role as well. Hamilton was named a major general and given the job of raising an army. By 1799, however, the risk of a war had shrunk, and Hamilton soon left his position.

The next year was an election year. Hamilton did not like either of the men running for president—Adams, a Federalist, and Jefferson. Hamilton supported another Federalist, Charles C. Pinckney, for the presidency. In the end, Jefferson and Aaron Burr were the final choices.

Aaron Burr (1756–1836)

Hamilton had known Burr for many years. They disliked each other's ideas, and they disliked each other personally. Hamilton decided to support Jefferson, believing Jefferson "was a lover of liberty." Burr, he said, "thinks of nothing but his own aggrandizement [power and reputation] and will be content with nothing short of permanent power in his own hands."

Because of a tie vote in the Electoral College, Congress had to decide the election of 1800. Jefferson won the vote, and Burr became the vice president. He knew Hamilton had opposed him. The personal war between Burr and Hamilton continued to grow.

In 1804, knowing that Jefferson would choose another man for vice president, Burr ran for governor of New York. Once again, Hamilton worked to defeat him. Hamilton still thought Burr would use political power to help only himself. Burr heard some of the things Hamilton publicly said about him and demanded that Hamilton apologize. When Hamilton refused,

Burr challenged him to a duel. Hamilton accepted.

Dueling had a long tradition in Europe and gained popu-larity in America during the Revolution. If one man felt another had insulted him, he could challenge the man to a duel. Refusing to accept the duel was seen as cowardly. Even when two men

Politicians, newspaper writers, and lawyers were often challenged to duels during the early days of the nation.

agreed to a duel, they were often able to settle their differences without actually fighting. Burr and Hamilton, however, could not.

On July 11, 1804, the two men rowed across the Hudson River and came ashore at Weehawken, New Jersey. Hamilton and Burr stood 10 large footsteps apart. Each held a pistol. When the command was given, each man took aim and fired. Hamilton's bullet missed—but Burr's aim was true. Hamilton slumped to the ground, fatally wounded. His friends rushed him back to New York for medical care, but there was nothing that could be done. The next day, Hamilton died. He was 49.

Many people attended Hamilton's funeral. They realized the important work he had done to help create the United States. Years later, the U.S. government honored him by putting his face on the $10 bill. Many modern historians have praised his work as well. The United States gained the power and wealth Hamilton hoped it would, thanks in part to his efforts.

Alexander Hamilton's grave at Trinity Church in Manhattan, New York

Glossary

artillery—large weapons, such as cannons, that require several soldiers to load, aim, and fire

Constitutional Congress—legislative assembly of delegates from the 13 colonies who met during and after the Revolutionary War; they issued the Declaration of Independence and wrote the Articles of Confederation

delegates—people at a meeting who represent a larger group of people

Electoral College—group of people who formally elect the U.S. president

finance—science or study of how money is made and spent

militia—citizens who have been organized to fight as a group but who are not professional soldiers

Parliament—part of the British government that makes laws

ratify—to formally approve

secretary—head of a government department

Did You Know?

- In 1785, Alexander Hamilton helped found a society to end slavery in New York.

- In 1794, farmers in Pennsylvania protested a tax on whiskey, which many of the farmers made from grains they grew. Hamilton and George Washington led a force of around 15,000 troops to Pennsylvania and ended the so-called Whiskey Rebellion.

- Although he was no longer in the government in 1796, Hamilton helped George Washington write the last speech he gave as president, called the Farewell Address.

- In 1801, Hamilton's oldest son Philip made fun of a man who had spoken out against his father and the Federalists. The men dueled, and Philip was killed.

- After killing Hamilton, Aaron Burr fled to Virginia and went into hiding. He finished his term as vice president and never faced a trial for killing Hamilton.

Timeline

1755	Born January 11 on the island of Nevis
1772	Arrives in Boston to begin his studies
1777	Joins the staff of General George Washington
1781	Leads a successful attack on the British at Yorktown, Virginia
1787	Attends the convention that drafts the Constitution; helps write *The Federalist Papers* in support of it
1789	Becomes the first secretary of the U.S. Treasury Department
1791	Promotes creation of the first national bank in the United States
1795	Leaves government service to practice law
1804	Dies after being wounded in a duel with Aaron Burr

Important People

Aaron Burr (1756–1836)
Like Alexander Hamilton, he joined the military at the beginning of the Revolutionary War and later became a lawyer in New York; he clashed with Hamilton over control of local and state politics in New York; he was accused of plotting to seize land from Spain and start a new country; he faced a trial in 1807 and was found innocent

Thomas Jefferson (1743–1826)
Third president of the United States, he served on the committee that wrote the Declaration of Independence and was the main author of that important document; he was also an inventor who created a new kind of plow and improved a device for writing two copies of a letter at once

James Madison (1751–1836)
Served as a lawmaker in Virginia and in Congress during the Revolution; many of his ideas were used to write the Constitution, and he is sometimes called the father of that document; he was elected the fourth U.S. president in 1809 and served for eight years

George Washington (1732–1799)
First saw military action fighting for the British during the French and Indian War (1754–1763); he was named commander of the American forces soon after the Revolutionary War began; he supported a stronger national government and served as the first president of the United States

Want to Know More?

More Books to Read

Boyd Higgins, Helen. *Alexander Hamilton, Young Statesman.* Carmel, Ind.: Patria Press, 2008.

McNeese, Tim. *Alexander Hamilton: Framer of the Constitution.* Philadelphia: Chelsea House Publishers, 2006.

Roberts, Russell. *The Life and Times of Thomas Jefferson.* Hockessin, Del.: Mitchell Lane Publishers, 2007.

Rosenberg, Pam. *Alexander Hamilton: Soldier and Statesman.* Chanhassen, Minn.: Child's World, 2004.

Santrey, Laurence, and JoAnn Early Macken. *George Washington: Founding Father.* New York: Scholastic, 2007.

Taylor-Butler, Christine. *The Constitution.* New York: Children's Press, 2008.

On the Web

For more information on this topic, use FactHound.

1. Go to *www.facthound.com*

2. Choose your grade level.

3. Begin your search.

This book's ID number is 9780756541163

FactHound will find the best sites for you.

On the Road

**U.S. Department of
the Treasury**
15 St. and Hamilton Place, N.W.
Washington, D.C. 20220
202/622-2000
The Treasury Building is
headquarters for the Office of
the Secretary of the Treasury.

Trinity Church
74 Trinity Place
New York, NY 10006
212/602-0800
Burial place of Alexander
Hamilton

Look for more We the People Biographies:

American Patriot: Benjamin Franklin

Civil War Spy: Elizabeth Van Lew

Confederate Commander: General Robert E. Lee

Confederate General: Stonewall Jackson

First of First Ladies: Martha Washington

A Signer for Independence: John Hancock

Union General and 18th President: Ulysses S. Grant

A complete list of We the People titles is available on our Web site:
www.compasspointbooks.com

Index

About the Author

Michael Burgan is a freelance writer of books for children and adults. A history graduate of the University of Connecticut, he has written more than 100 fiction and nonfiction children's books. For adult audiences, he has written news articles, essays, and plays. Michael Burgan is a recipient of an Educational Press Association of America award.